THE
CALLIGRAPHIC ART
OF
ARTHUR BAKER

THE
CALLIGRAPHIC ART
OF
ARTHUR BAKER

WITH AN INTRODUCTION BY

WILLIAM HOGARTH

CHARLES SCRIBNER'S SONS · NEW YORK

Library of Congress Cataloging in Publication Data

Baker, Arthur.
The calligraphic art of Arthur Baker.

1. Baker, Arthur.   2. Calligraphy—Technique.
3. Art, Abstract.   I. Title.
NK3631.B34A4   1983   745.6'1'0924   82-42648
ISBN 0-684-17837-0

1 3 5 7 9 11 13 15 17 19   Q/C   20 18 16 14 12 10 8 6 4 2

Printed in the United States of America.

INTRODUCTION

Arthur Baker is the most innovative and accomplished master of letters working today. He published his first book, called, simply, *Calligraphy,* just ten years ago. In that ground-breaking work, the late Tommy Thompson, himself a master scribe, wrote, "Baker weaves his script on a fanciful and magic loom from his personal and endless patterns. . . . In his art he's a natural. . . . In this most beautiful calligraphy, rhythm, letter design, and disciplined composition are accomplished without showing human effort. Character refinement in the person of the writer will always be evident in this expression of art and joy."

There have been more than a dozen books since then, but that first book of Baker's innovative letterforms and abstractions was a breakthrough in the somewhat special and conservative world of calligraphy. Its effect, worldwide, has been enormously influential in the virtual explosion of interest in the art and craft of beautiful writing today.

With this book it is clear that Arthur Baker's art has come into its own. In the light of this work, art critics and historians will have to be more precise in their use of the word *calligraphic* as a cliché reference to an artist's use of linear detail. This work is true calligraphy and true art. The images, created in a diversity of styles, all stem from letters and express a free, joyous playfulness and delight in turning our twenty-six letters into visual music, complete with themes, variations, fugues.

There is a sampling here of dozens of approaches to letters as art, each in turn representative of hundreds of experiments. White cut-paper images on dark grounds are snipped from folded papers, like children's paper dolls; since each is based on a single letter, their opening, flower-like, into mandalas and tondos of involuted letterforms gives pleasure to the sophisticated, mathematically minded child in all of us. Science and art mesh as well in pages that seem like notes for the architecture of unknown worlds. The graphic imagination of these plates suggests links with primitive masks, totems, atavistic magic icons, but in their sophistication and abstraction they are truly avant-garde.

But it is not at all necessary to approach the art of Arthur Baker intellectually. We can simply take delight in his obvious pleasure in creating the flowing and staccato pen and brush forms on each page, then let our fancy take over. On close study, however, Baker's abstractions disclose their basis in some component of a letter of the alphabet: a delicate serif, overlays of strong vertical stems, curved forms overlapping, massings of letters written one over the other to suggest pictographs from an unknown language, poems from Saturn, telegrams from Stonehenge.

Arthur Baker has had a lifelong curiosity about the form and structure of our letters. It led him to investigate the origins of the great Roman capitals—those cold, pristine, carved letters still to be seen on monuments in the Mediterranean world—which, after two thousand years, are still the basis of all our writing and, indeed, all our transmitted learning. Baker wondered how the ancient scribes created the letters before the cutters V-shaped them into marble and limestone. Working backward from manuscripts of the third century and studying the written letters on the walls of Pompeii, he deduced the system of manipulated pen and brush strokes that gave shape and proportion to the great *capitalis monumentalis* of the first century. Only a hand as sympathetic to letter strokes as that of Arthur Baker could have made the discovery. He found what Leonardo and Dürer had sought during the Renaissance: a pattern and method of manipulating the pen and brush to create a rhythmic series of strokes. The Renaissance masters had clouded the issue with attempts to prove that the Roman letters were formed with compass and square, and their drawings continue to befuddle novice scribes today.

To teach the original formation of these letters, Baker has created a series of instructional manuals, each demonstrating stroke-by-stroke, one letter to a page, the pen manipulation needed to convey the humanistic genius of the historic alphabets. This is in keeping with his own rigorous discipline at capturing a gestural line. He has also been responsible for designing hundreds of typefaces based on calligraphy, beginning with his prize-winning *Baker Signet*—a perennial favorite of architects, art directors, and commercial designers. His credentials as a master of letterform are impeccable, his manuals are unique, and his imagination has no boundaries. If Arthur Baker has no peers, it is largely due to the failure of other calligraphers to follow him in his quest for excellence, to go beyond craft into serious innovative creativity.

Baker's influence is prodigal, and he is generous with appearances at lecture/demonstrations, gathering admirers as loyal as those who know his ideas only from books. The excitement, the creativity, and the art of Arthur Baker are all uniquely American. His adherents form a group practicing what can be truly called the New American Calligraphy, recognized as such throughout the world.

To look closely at the pages that follow is to surrender to the communicative power of Arthur Baker's art. This art can fire the sympathetic mind, and it should at the very least stimulate calligraphers to see in a fresh way how very exciting the twenty-six symbols of our common heritage can be.

Keep in mind, as you turn these pages, that even the most abstract images evolve from letters; that a stroke component of a letterform in pen or brush has become art, but remains also inescapably calligraphy. Perhaps my favorite reminder of this is Plate 35: two long-tailed, juxtaposed *G*'s that are, in their elegant simplicity, reminiscent of Picasso's reduction of the image of the bull to its essential outline. The ancient Phoenicians were among the first people to organize a written alphabet, and the bull, *aleph,* became the letter *A.* The Greeks adapted it as *alpha,* added *B, beta*—and alpha-beta became alphabet. We have perhaps come full circle. In the art of Arthur Baker we see alpha-beta merge in the art of letters, in letters as art. It is tempting to see whole worlds in these abstract images based on the tools of human communication. But it is also sufficient to look, to absorb, to be present at this visual feast.

WILLIAM HOGARTH
Sea Cliff, New York

Plate 1

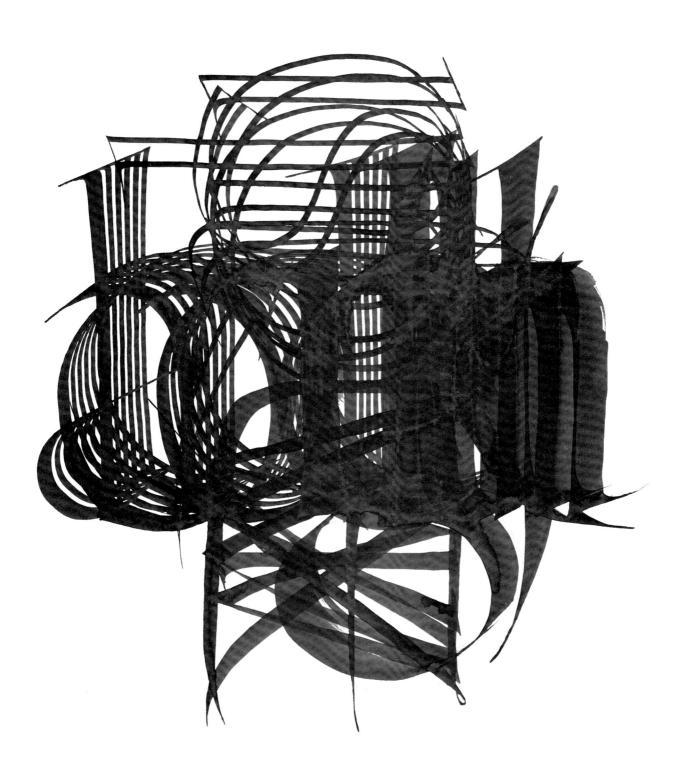

Plate 2

Plate 3

Plate 4

Plate 5

Plate 6

Plate 7

Plate 8

Plate 9

Plate 10

abcdefghijk
lmnopqrst uvw
xyz

arthur baker 1982

Plate 11

Plate 12

Plate 13

Plate 14

Plate 15

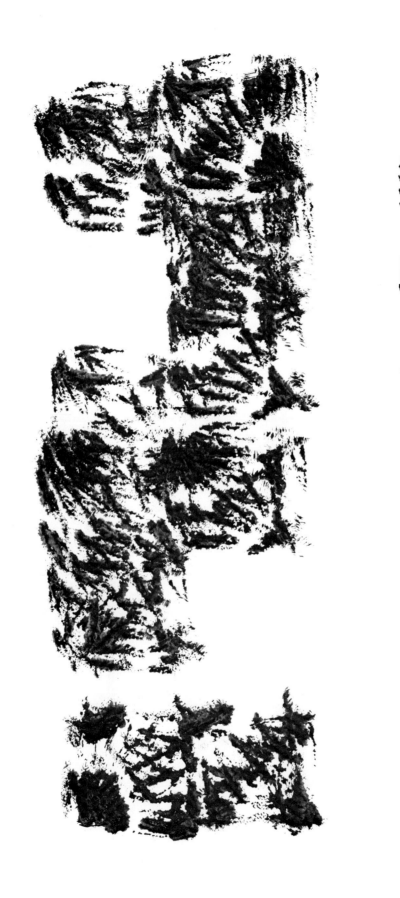

Plate 16

Plate 17

Plate 18

Plate 19

Plate 20

Plate 21

Plate 22

Plate 23

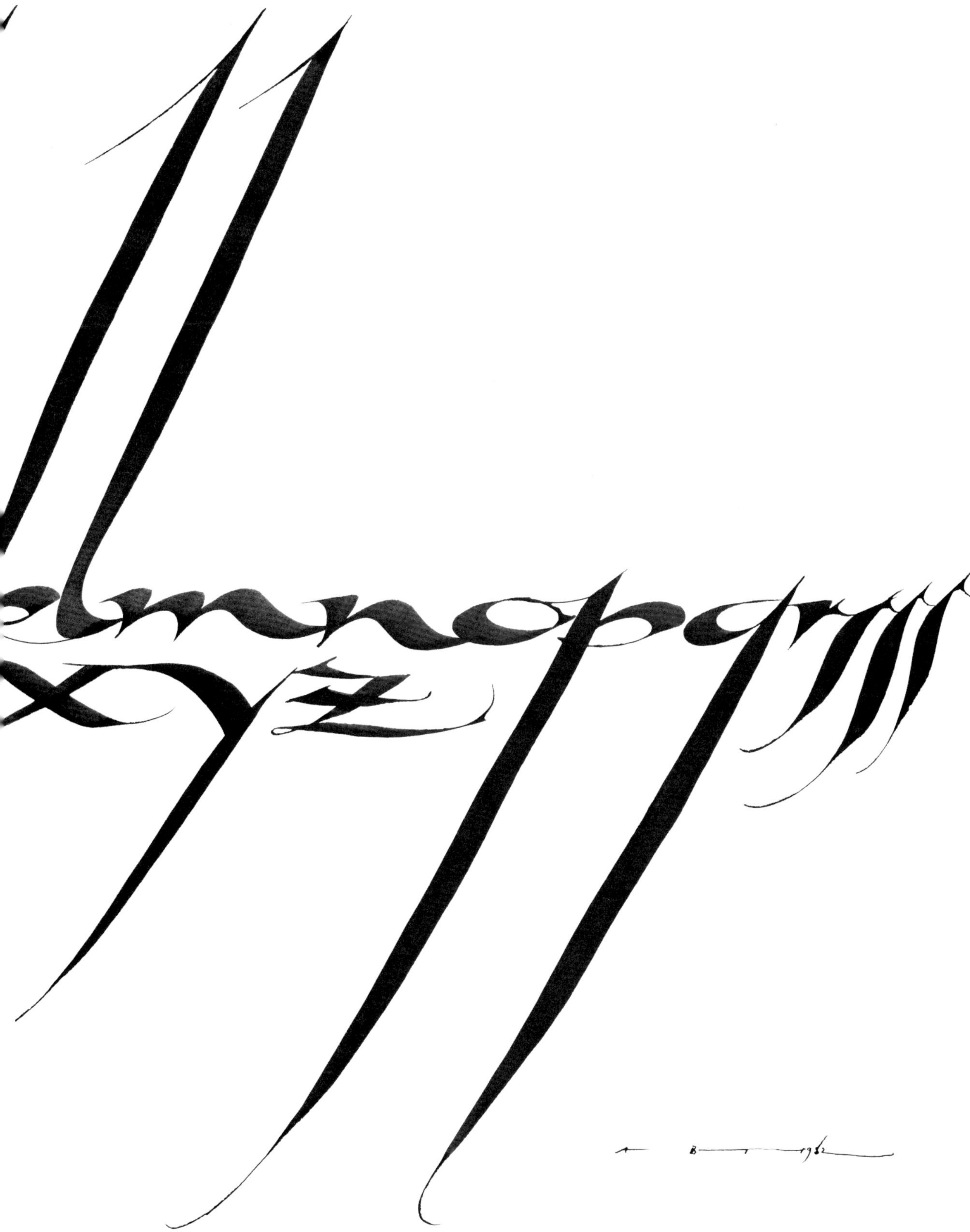

Plate 24

Plate 25

Plate 26

Plate 27

Plate 28

arthur baker 1982

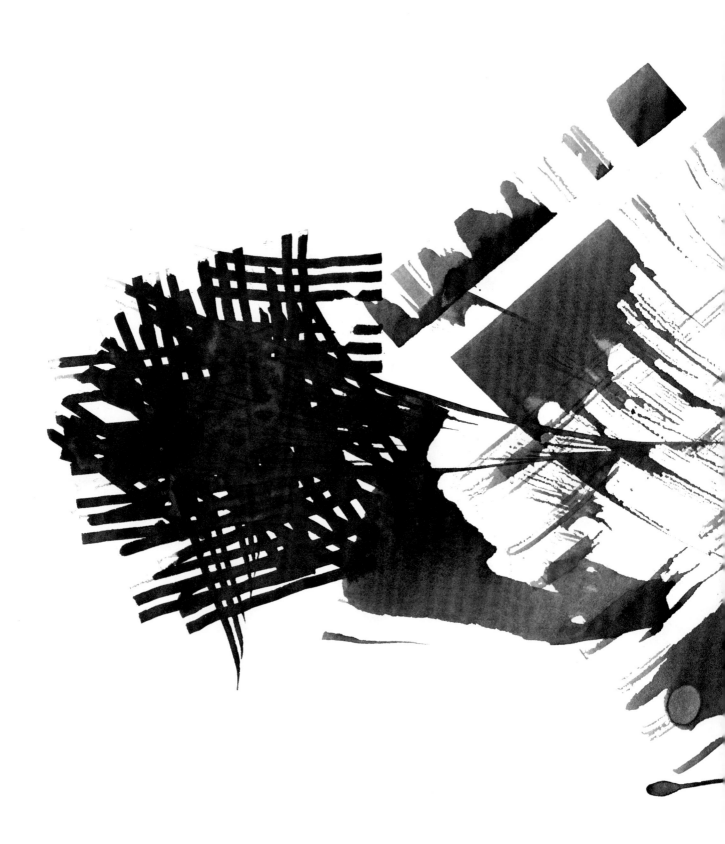

Plate 29

Plate 30

arthur baker
1982

Plate 31

Plate 36

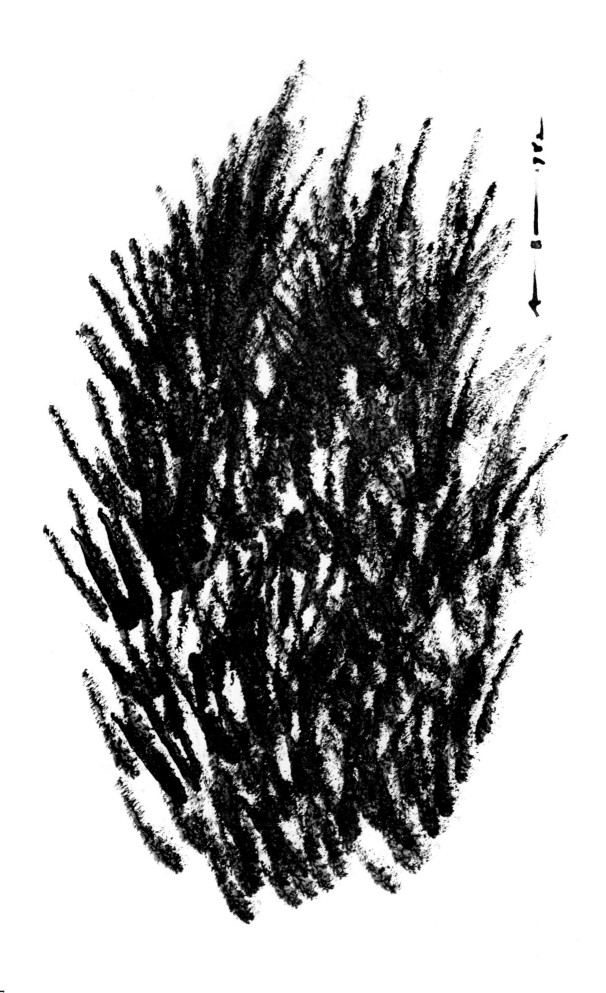

Plate 37

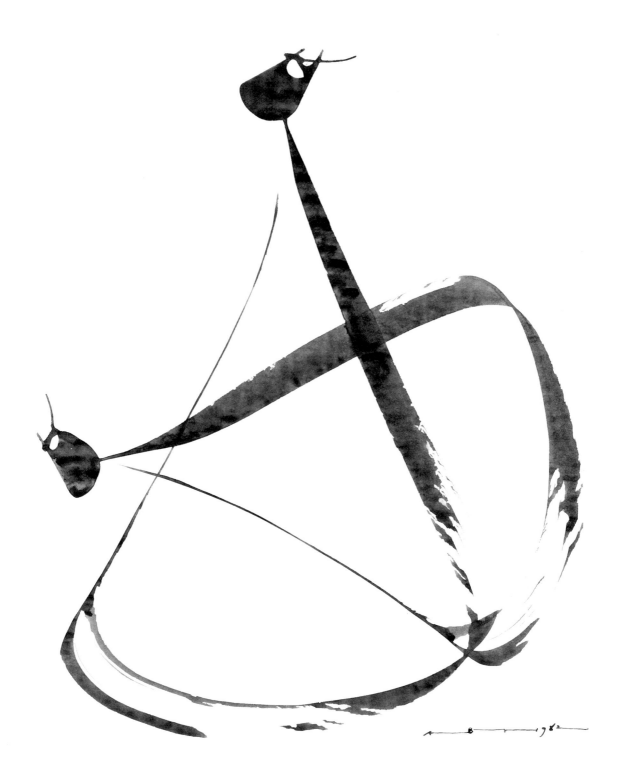

Plate 35

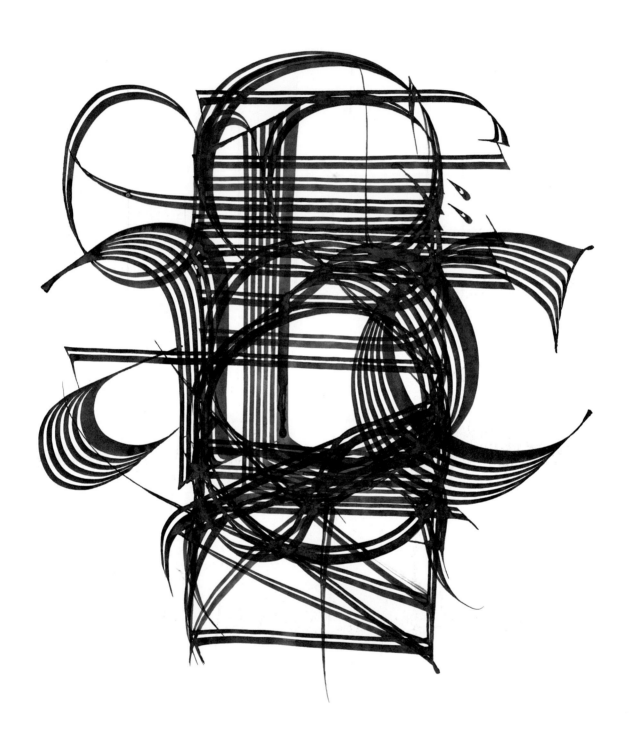

Plate 34

Plate 33

Plate 32

Plate 38

Plate 39

Plate 40

Plate 41

Plate 42

Plate 43

Plate 44

Plate 45

Notes on the Plates

Arthur Baker uses a variety of tools in his work, but essentially a battery of handmade pens—wide brass nibs that move effortlessly on the page because of their buffed edges. He has designed many of these himself, including dozens of split-nib, multiple-line pens in innovative spacings and widths. Most of the abstract images in this book were created with flat brushes using ink and gouache, either in a dry-brush technique or fluid watercolor style. The original art was executed at slightly more than twice the size shown here, generally at great speed.

1. The *quadrata* alphabet, written quickly with the nib running dry on occasion, showing the striations of the pen nib.
2. Solid and thinned ink with the broad pen, including a multiline nib with one edge weighted.
3. A wide pen alphabet, freely written to create a bold unity on the page, a sculptural mass.
4. Component strokes common to the Roman capitals treated abstractly and overwritten for textural effect.
5. A cut-paper design based on the letter *I*. White flint paper was folded in quarters and cut through the layers with a blade, then pasted on black background paper.
6. Created with a weighted, multiline pen, overlaid for pattern effect.
7. A letter stroke accenting a basic calligraphic left curve, multiplied into a rondo of movement with several pens.
8. Brushed gouache, with letter strokes marshaled in blocks.
9. A multiline pen, one side weighted, used to stress the variations of the turned meeting strokes of letters *A* and *V*, overwritten into a shaped triangular pattern.
10. A battalion of small *D* letters surrounds a minuscule alphabet, all in flat pens, with ink solid and thinned.
11. Bold, brush-drawn forms in thinned ink suggest the monolithic stone circles of Stonehenge and Avebury.
12. An octagonal form created with solid and multiline pens from stroke components of Roman capitals, in thinned ink.
13. Overlaid letter strokes in solid and multiline pens.
14. A trefoil design based on the letter *J*, cut from layers of white paper, then unfolded and mounted on black backing paper.
15. A tour-de-force in thinned and solid ink. The staccato strokes of the multiline pen suggest an affinity to Kandinsky.
16. The pattern of dry-brush gouache forms could almost be pictographs.
17. The turned brush, like the turned pen—letter components become natural forms in this gouache.
18. A multiline pen created the alphabet; the rough *O* forms were dry-brushed in with the edge of a household sponge.
19. An amoebic, microcosmic pattern of letter strokes, in broad pens.
20. Crossings of letter components, freely brushed in gouache.
21. One broad pen, twirled in a nontraditional manner between thumb and forefinger, was used to create this alphabet. A rough-hewn, almost sculptural mass is the result.
22. Atavistic nature forms in gouache, brush-drawn.
23. An elegant alphabet in broad pen, radically turned, written fast.
24. Multiline and solid pens, with an overwritten alphabet framed between the split-nib *A* and *Z*.
25. A cut-paper triad—kaleidoscopic results from the letter *J*, blade-cut when folded, opened and mounted on black backing paper.

26. The weighted multiline pen, plus a single-weight nib, tumbles the Roman alphabet into an octagonal shape.
27. An octagon containing Roman capitals, over-written with the wide pen.
28. Stuttering repeats of letters within the alphabet, smoothly executed with a single-weight pen.
29. All forms are ink-drawn with pens; the exploded letter-stroke components suggest early Russian constructivist art.
30. A playful pun on *P*s and *Q*s—the forest of bold thinned-ink forms massed above an elegant, pen-turned alphabet.
31. Solid and multiline pens mass the alphabet in a cruciform.
32. Many nibs, split and solid, alternate to create a handsome foundational Roman alphabet.
33. A masklike form, composed of densely over-written letterforms, in several broad pens, with thinned and solid ink.
34. Overlaid small letters, written with various split-nib pens, present the alphabet in a new light.
35. The elegance and economy of the pen-drawn crossed minuscule *G* forms suggest the simplicity of Picasso's bull drawings.
36. An organic form, simply brushed in gouache.
37. Brush strokes reflective of tapering letter-forms become pine-needle massings in this gouache painting.
38. Explosive brush strokes again suggest the most primitive, basic natural shapes.
39. A highly sophisticated overlaid turning of split-nib pens in running-dry fashion, based on letter and figure forms.
40. Bold letterforms made with one broad pen build a cage of alphabetic strength in this ink drawing.
41. A flowing pen-drawn alphabet, with repeat letters; the wavering upward strokes of the minuscule *D*s are in delicate contrast to the forward motion of the other letters.
42. *A B C D* in bold *quadrata* letters surround a massed overlay of other capital forms, in various pens.
43. Dry-brush and fluid gouache suggest an involuted natural form.
44. All are logical pen strokes in this solid- and thinned-ink composition, but their abstraction is startling.
45. A leaf, a fossil, a mineral geode all come to mind from the artist's massing of letter strokes in gouache.